D0791620

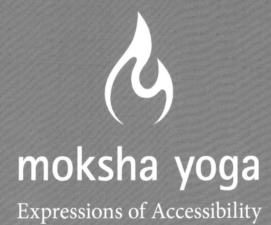

moksha yoga

Expressions of Accessibility

Printed in Canada.

ISBN 978-0-9867563-0-6

ENVIRONMENTAL BENEFITS STATEMENT

Moksha Yoga Winnipeg saved the following
resources by printing the pages of this book on
chlorine free paper made with 60% post-consumer
waste.

TREES	WATER	SOLID WASTE	GREENHOUSE GASES
18	8,406	510	1,745
FULLY GROWN	GALLONS	POUNDS	POUNDS

Calculations based on research by Environmental Defense and the Paper Task Force.
Manufactured at Friesens Corporation

Foreword

Every yoga practice can be strengthened by connecting to the root of a posture and an intention for practice. The length and grace of the spine is uncovered when we find our rooting in the feet. The mind settles when a strong intention is set as the fuel for practice.

The Moksha community operates in exactly the same way. We root our practice on and off the mat with Seven Pillars. They are intentions that we share in effort to support each other in a life of learning and growth.

Our Seven Pillars are:
Be Healthy – We work to support lifelong health for the body and mind
Be Accessible – We endeavour to be accessible in our language, postures, and systems
Live Green – We live to protect and serve the natural world
Sangha Support – We believe in the power of community
Outreach – We use our creativity and effort to help others
Live to Learn – We commit to lifelong learning
Be Peace – We offer the benefit of our practice to the benefit of all beings everywhere

Symbolically these Seven Pillars stand in a circle and unite every Moksha student and teacher. The postures are practiced not by hired models but by members of the Winnipeg community who share our view that yoga is alive and continuous, inside and outside the studio walls.

What MYW has done with this book reflects what every Moksha practitioner is doing— working hard, sweating lots, and caring deeply about creating a more peaceful, fun, healthy, creative, inspired world one posture at a time. To us, that in itself is inspiring!

The book is printed on 80% recycled paper (60% post-consumer waste) and the proceeds of the book benefit youth art programs around the globe.

Jessica Robertson and Ted Grand
Co-Founders, Moksha Yoga

Expressions of Accessibility *(about this book)*

The participants of this book are not yoga models, but each is a wonderful model of yoga. They are all members of the Moksha Yoga Winnipeg community and each have a committed yoga practice. Knowing this, we asked them to simply shine in their posture.

The photos will take you through the 90-minute Moksha series. We offered zero instruction for the shoot, we had no make-up crew, we just had a hot room and committed participants. It was tempting to instruct, "Drop that hip a little, now lift your chin a little, shine from your fingertips." However, we felt offering tips on how to make it look better for a 'picture' would have removed us from the purpose of this book.

So here you are, great people sharing their yoga, expressing their accessibility of the Moksha Practice. Enjoy, celebrate, and see you soon in the hot room!

Phil and Ryann Doucette
Director and Owners, Moksha Yoga Winnipeg

Purpose of Book

Yoga is accessible to everyone—creativity should be too.

One of the most important pillars in Moksha is COMMUNITY. Every studio offers Karma classes where students can practice yoga by donation. Each month studios share those Karma funds with charities and non-profit groups in their communities.

This project is a non-profit initiative, a karma collective with all proceeds going to support youth art programs around the globe. With each sale of the book, funds go directly to art supplies, instruction, and resources that will help youth access the enriching benefits of arts and culture.

Gratitude

Possibility comes alive with community. This book came together with the vision, hard work, and commitment of many people. We bow with deep gratitude to celebrate the community who made this book happen:

Moksha Founders Jess and Ted, Photographer Casey Harrison and his team, the staff and energy exchangers at Moksha Winnipeg, all the students who shared their practice for this shoot, Tripwire Media, our Graphic Designer Kiery Drysdale, Winnipeg Art Gallery, and finally, every Moksha studio who supported the making and vision of this book.

Mountain *(Tadasana)*

Through alignment, stamina, but mostly breath, practicing yoga has increased my endurance for long rehearsals and performances.

—*Simon, Violinist, Winnipeg Symphony*

Breathing *(Pranayama)*

Yoga has helped me cultivate a calm centre and place of peace
that I can draw on when work becomes challenging.

—*Erin, Social Worker*

Tree Pose *(Vrksasana)*

We discovered Karma classes as strangers,
and now practice together as friends.

—*Abeth, Ray, Reggie, Best Friends*

Crescent Moon
(Ardha Chandrasana)

I discovered new ways to reach and teach my students.

—Kimberley, Elementary School Teacher, and Breena

Powerful Pose *(Utkatasana)*

With 23 years experience, I can tell you that I wish I had discovered yoga so much earlier in my career. It has given me a sense of balance both physically and mentally that allows me to feel prepared for just about everything—in a job where I need to be ready for anything.

—Damian, Police Officer

Awkward Pose
(Utkatasana II)

My yoga connected me deeper to my movement.
I learned to truly dance from my SOUL.

—Jennifer, Dancer, Royal Winnipeg Ballet

Eagle Pose
(Garudasana)

After every Moksha class, I am able to say to myself: There you are! I am reintroduced every time.

—*Lisa, TV/Movie Producer*

Prayer Twist
(Parivritta Utkatasana)

In sharing our practice together, we've discovered new ways to love each other.

—*Sean and Geni, Husband and Wife*

Backbend

My yoga helps me start the day so my mind is clear and open to all possibilities. Having a daily physical practicc helps me carry a calm, yogic frame of mind throughout the day.

—Joy, Childcare

Runners Lunge *(Banarasana)*

The combination of stretching, endurance, and cross-training have been a godsend to our busy work schedules and desire to continue running competitively. We're addicted to yoga!

—Dave and Tammy, Armed Forces

Warrior 1
(Virabhadrasana 1)

I discovered that my breath can foster a
compassionate response instead of a reaction.

—*John, Art Dealer*

Warrior 2 *(Virabhadrasana ll)*

I just had a milestone birthday and feel with the help of yoga that I will reach many more.

—Marcia

Living with Rheumatoid arthritis, Moksha Yoga helped lubricate my joints and improve my overall health. And so much more.

—Bev

Best Friends

Triangle
(Trikonasana)

Rob and I work very physical jobs. We've found the greatest benefit in Moksha is the ability to calm the mind and body with breath.

—*Rob and Laura, Public Works Foreman/Firefighter*

Forward Bend *(Padangustasana)*

Yoga and breathing have created stability in my pottery, and in my life. If I am still, my work is still.

—Lane, Potter

Wide Legged Forward Bend
(Prasarita Padotanasana)

Yoga began as a means to physically work my body, and in the process, changed my life. While I continue to love the physical practice of asana, yoga has opened in me confidence, compassion, and balance.

—Shauna, Studio Manager, Moksha Yoga Winnipeg

Runners Lunge II *(Banarasana II)*

Yoga helps me to see the ego in myself and in others. To recognize your ego as part of you but not "you" has been a major discovery and the practice of yoga has been a large part of this realization. For the first time in my life I feel space around my mind.

—Len, Cinematographer

Toppling Tree
(Patanvriksasana)

Yoga has taught me that life isn't about being the best, but about helping others be their best.

—Amelia, Tri-Athelete

Dancers Pose *(Natarajasana)*

Before I started doing yoga, I never looked in the mirror.
My practice helped me accept and even love my body just
the way it is. Yoga has helped me to really know myself
and to see that I can do things I didn't think were possible.

—*Julia, Accountant*

Corpse Pose *(Savasana)*

Yoga has helped me THRIVE in my battle against Cancer.

—Michelle, Cancer Survivor

Wind Relieving
(Pavana Muktasana)

Yoga has helped me develop strength, flexibility,
and an overall sense of wellness.

—Nicola, Nursing Assistant

Leg Lift *(Jatharasana)*

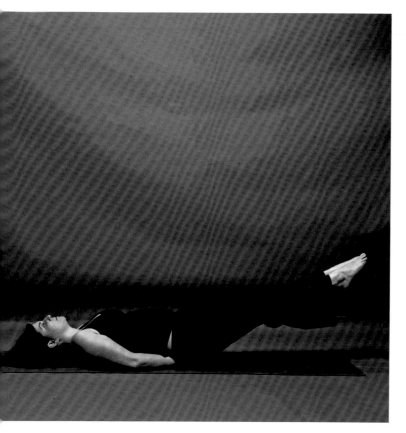

Through yoga, I've learned that the smallest changes
make the biggest difference.

—*Emily, Journalist*

Bridge Pose
(Setu Bandhasana)

I discovered body awareness.

—Joe, Real Estate Developer

Cobra Pose  *(Bhujangasana)*

As I begin every class I remember a teacher's profound advice, "5 billion people in the world; 5 billion practices. Make this practice your own." And so I do.

—*Janet, Director of Sales Training and Development*

Locust Pose *(Salabhasana)*

Yoga has helped me realize the power of intention. If we all thought the purest of intentions—the world would be a wonderful place.

—Kameron, Trainer, Financial Services

Full Locust *(Poorna Salabhasana)*

My body is healing itself. I am playing soccer again and have a larger range of physical activity in my life from competitive to relaxing, exciting to calming! Thank you yoga!

—*Aisha, Life Coach*

Bow Pose *(Dhanurasana)*

Being present with wonderful conscious breaths that
allow me the courage to explore and express who I am
in everyday life is something that I am truly grateful for.

—Richard, Firefighter

Child's Pose *(Balasana)*

I always used to focus on the outside first. With my yoga practice, I discovered myself from the inside.

—Erica, Nursing Student

Downward Dog
(Adho Mukha Svanasana)

Plank Pose

Four-Limbed Staff Pose
(Chaturanga Dandasana)

Upward Facing Dog
*(Urdhva Mukha
Svanasana)*

Downward Dog
(Adho Mukha Svanasana)

I discovered how to connect with myself and quiet my feelings
of competition, anxiety, and anticipation.

Lisa, Boxer

Sleeping Hero
(Supta Virasana)

I discovered my life's work.

—*Leslie, MYW Teacher*

Camel Pose
(Ustrasana)

I uncovered GRATITUDE. I am
grateful for my body's capacity,
and less interested in how it looks.

—Tara, Psychology Graduate Student

Pigeon Pose
(Eka Pada Kapotasana)

I discovered that I don't have to live with back pain.
I literally found new freedom in my life.

—*Casey, Photographer*

Rabbit Pose
(Sasangasana)

The work that happens on the mat has helped me
become the person I've always wanted to be.

—Clancy, MYW Teacher

Seated Side Twist
(Parivritta Janu Shirsasana)

My practice purifies my perception.

—Nena, MYW Teacher

Seated Forward Bend
(Paschimottanasana)

I discovered the power of 'WE", the potential of "US."

—*Ryann, MYW Owner/Director*

Spinal Twist
(Ardha Matsyendrasana)

We've honestly discovered how to retire.

Tom and Janet, Retired

Cobblers Pose
(Badakonasana)

Yoga makes me grateful for what I have and makes
me want to live the best life I can!

—*Shauna, Pediatric Nurse*

Skull Shining Breath *(Kapalabhati)*

With yoga we discovered new voices: we're calmer on stage, we sing with more support from our breath, and off stage we're more open and inspired in our songwriting.

—Keith and Renee, Musicians

Corpse Pose
(Savasana)